Introduction

Ice cream is one of the most favorite desserts for both children and adults; and the best way to cool off on a hot summer day! Cook your homemade ice cream and treat your family and friends with delicious sweet and refreshing dessert.
There are several ways to cook ice cream:

- Use special ice cream maker or other freezing appliance to mix ingredients and freeze your ice cream

- Combine your favorite toppings: fruit, chocolate, berries, syrups. Follow the easiest instructions in this book and create your own gorgeous summer dessert!

Now let's see the variety of existing frozen desserts and their difference:

- Frozen Yogurt - is a light refreshing dessert with a slightly sour taste. The main ingredient in this dessert is yogurt, so it is a low-calorie and cultured milk product with a minimum fat. Really healthy and tasty idea for summer!

- Ice Cream – is a classic frozen dessert made from milk, cream, butter, sugar and different toppings. You can make it with chocolate or coffee, fruit or berries. Any kind of ice cream is delicious! But be careful if you watch your figure – it is a caloric product.

- Gelato – is a low-fat analog to classic ice cream. It is a popular Italian frozen dessert made from fresh cow's milk, cream and sugar, with berries, nuts, chocolate and fresh fruits.

- Sorbet – is a frozen dessert made from sugar syrup and fruit juice. It is a simply and quickly dessert without the use of diary products.

- Granita – ia a Sicilian dessert with crushed fruit ice and sugar. It is a variety of sorbets, but has a more dense structure. Perfect idea for summer parties and picnics! You can also cook it with alcohol to make a crazy cocktail!

Enjoy your summer with refreshing recipes!

Table of Content

Introduction 1
Table of Content.. 3
Frozen Yogurt 6
    Blueberry Frozen Yogurt 6
    Apple-Pie Frozen Yogurt 7
    Classic Vanilla Frozen Yogurt 8
    Tropical Frozen Yogurt 9
    Chocolate Frozen Yogurt with Peanut Butter 10
    Frozen Rhubarb Yogurt 11
    Chili Mango Frozen Yogurt.. 12
    New York Cheesecake Frozen Yogurt 13
    Kiwi Frozen Yogurt 14
    Baileys Frozen Yogurt 15
Ice Cream... 16
    Chocolate Crisps Coffee Ice Cream 16
    Simple Vanilla Ice Cream 17
    Drunk Avocado Ice Cream 18
    Ricotta Hazelnut Ice Cream... 20
    Blueberry Ice Cream.. 21
    Fried Mexican Ice Cream 22
    Pumpkin Ice Cream 24
    Green Tea Ice Cream.. 25
    Vegetarian Banana Ice Cream 26
    Salted Caramel Ice Cream 27
Gelato.. 29

Berry Mint Gelato...29

Limoncello Gelato..31

Honey Gelato...33

Coconut Banana Gelato 35

Tiramisu Gelato 36

Coffee Gelato with Orange 38

Choco-Choco Gelato 40

Caramel Gelato with White Chocolate...41

Melon Gelato with Amaretto 43

Spicy Cinnamon Gelato 45

Sorbets..46

Fresh Green Apple Sorbet..46

Pineapple Daiquiri Sorbet...48

Mojito Sorbet 49

Sweet Tomato-Basil Sorbet..50

Mint Espresso Sorbet 51

Strawberry Balsamic Sorbet...52

Romantic Lavender Sorbet...53

Grapefruit'n'Rum Sorbet..54

Cherry Vanilla Sorbet 55

Summer Citrus Sorbet...56

Granita 57

Green Tea Granita..57

Citrus Ginger Granita...58

Watermelon Granita 59

Strawberry Basil Granita...60

Cappuccino Granita..61

- Peach Granita 62
- Champagne Granita 63
- Margarita Granita 64
- Pinacolada Granita 65
- Chocolate Mint Granita 66

Credits 67

Frozen Yogurt

Blueberry Frozen Yogurt

- ✓ 2 cups plain low-fat yogurt
- ✓ 2 cups fresh blueberries
- ✓ 1 firm banana, cut
- ✓ 2 tbsp. sugar or honey
- ✓ 1 tsp. lime juice
- ✓ 1/2 tsp. lime zest

Blend all ingredients in a food processor, make sure that the sugar is dissolved. Use an ice cream maker according to instructions to make frozen yogurt, or pour the mixture into a covered container and let freeze for at least 90 minutes prior to eating. Before serving keep frozen yogurt at cool room temperature for not being too hard. Garnish with fresh blueberries.

Apple-Pie Frozen Yogurt

- ✓ 2 cups plain Greek yogurt
- ✓ 1/2 cup heavy cream
- ✓ 1 large firm golden apple, peeled and cut
- ✓ 1/2 cup honey
- ✓ 2 tsp ground cinnamon

In food processor, puree apple until smooth, blend in yogurt, honey and cinnamon. Use an ice cream maker according to instructions to make frozen yogurt, or pour the mixture into a covered container and let freeze for at least 90 minutes prior to eating. Before serving keep frozen yogurt at cool room temperature for not being too hard. Garnish with apple slices and honey.

Classic Vanilla Frozen Yogurt

- ✓ 2 cups plain low-fat yogurt
- ✓ 1/2 cup sugar
- ✓ 1/2 tsp. vanilla

Mix or blend all ingredients. Make the sugar dissolve. Taste, add in as much sugar as seems good to you. Use an ice cream maker according to instructions to make vanilla yogurt, or pour the mixture into a covered container and let freeze for at least 90 minutes prior to eating. Before serving keep frozen yogurt at cool room temperature for not being too hard.

Tropical Frozen Yogurt

- ✓ 2 cups plain low-fat Greek yogurt
- ✓ 1 tbsp. coconut cream
- ✓ 1/2 cup sugar
- ✓ 1/2 tsp. vanilla
- ✓ 1 cup fresh pineapple, finely cut
- ✓ 2 tbsp. coconut, grated
- ✓ 1 1/2 tbsp. Malibu rum

Blend the yogurt, sugar, coconut cream, vanilla and rum, make sure that the sugar is dissolved. In a big bowl combine yogurt mixture with pineapple and grated coconut. Use an ice cream maker according to instructions to make frozen yogurt, or pour the mixture into a covered container and let freeze for at least 90 minutes prior to eating. Defrost slightly before serving.

Chocolate Frozen Yogurt with Peanut Butter

- ✓ 2 cups plain or vanilla low-fat yogurt
- ✓ 1/2 cup semi-sweet chocolate chips
- ✓ 3 tbsp. white chocolate chips
- ✓ 1/3 cup creamy peanut butter
- ✓ 1/3 cup brown sugar
- ✓ 1/3 heavy cream

In saucepan, combine the sugar, cream and chocolate chips. Stir over low heat until sugar and chocolate chips melted. Let the chocolate sauce cool a bit, then add peanut butter and yogurt. After the mixture is completely cool - add white chocolate chips and mix thoroughly. Use an ice cream maker according to instructions to make frozen yogurt, or pour the mixture into a covered container and let freeze for at least 90 minutes prior to eating. Defrost slightly before serving. Garnish with melted chocolate or whipped cream.

Frozen Rhubarb Yogurt

- ✓ 2 cups rhubarb, chopped
- ✓ 1/2 cup ripe strawberry jam
- ✓ 2 cups plain or low-fat yogurt
- ✓ 1/2 cup sugar
- ✓ 2 tsp. fresh mint finely chopped

In saucepan, combine rhubarb, strawberry jam and sugar. Cook until rhubarb is soft, then transfer it in a food processor or blender and puree rhubarb to make it smooth. Let it cool. Pour the rhubarb mixture in a big bowl, mix with yogurt and mind. Use an ice cream maker according to instructions to make frozen yogurt, or pour the mixture into a covered container and let freeze for at least 90 minutes prior to eating. Defrost slightly before serving. Garnish with fresh mint leaves or fresh strawberries.

Chili Mango Frozen Yogurt

- ✓ 2 cups plain low-fat Greek yogurt
- ✓ 2 cups fresh ripe mangoes, peeled and diced
- ✓ 1/2 cup coconut milk
- ✓ 1/2 teaspoon chili powder
- ✓ 1/2 cup icing sugar

Place mango, yogurt, coconut milk, chili powder and icing sugar in a food processor, and blend until smooth. Use an ice cream maker according to instructions to make frozen yogurt, or pour the mixture into a covered container and let freeze for at least 90 minutes prior to eating. Defrost slightly before serving. Garnish with mango slices and chili flakes.

New York Cheesecake Frozen Yogurt

- ✓ 2 cups plain low-fat yogurt
- ✓ 1 cup Philadelphia cream cheese, softened
- ✓ 1/2 cup heavy cream
- ✓ 1 cup icing sugar
- ✓ 1/2 tsp. vanilla extract
- ✓ Cherry pie filling
- ✓ Graham crackers

Mix cream cheese, yogurt, icing sugar, vanilla extract with mixer or food processor on medium speed until well blended. Blend in heavy cream. Use an ice cream maker according to instructions to make frozen yogurt, or pour the mixture into a covered container and let freeze for at least 90 minutes prior to eating. Defrost for about 20 minutes before serving. Garnish with cherry pie filling and graham crackers.

Kiwi Frozen Yogurt

- ✓ 2 cups plain low-fat Greek yogurt
- ✓ 1/2 cup ripe kiwi, chopped
- ✓ 2 tbsp. lime juice
- ✓ 2 tsp. lime zest
- ✓ 1 cup icing sugar
- ✓ kiwi and lime slices

Make a Kiwi fruit puree: blend kiwi, lime juice, lime zest and icing sugar until smooth. Mix kiwi puree with yogurt; transfer it into the ice cream maker and make frozen yogurt according to instructions. You can also pour the kiwi mixture into a covered container and let freeze for at least 90 minutes prior to eating. Defrost frozen yogurt for about 20 minutes before serving. Garnish with kiwi and lime slices, if yogurt isn't sweet enough garnish with honey.

Baileys Frozen Yogurt

- ✓ 2 cups vanilla Greek yogurt
- ✓ 2 tbsp. light corn syrup
- ✓ 2 tbsp. Nutella, melted
- ✓ 1/2 cup Baileys Irish Cream
- ✓ 1/3 cup brown sugar
- ✓ 2 tbsp. hazelnut

Place hazelnuts and sugar in a food processor, blend until crumbs. Add corn syrup, Nutella, Baileys Irish Cream. Mix it well, be sure that the sugar is dissolved. Transfer sweet syrup into a big bowl, combine it with yogurt. Put mixture into the ice cream maker and make frozen yogurt according to instructions. You can also pour it into a covered container and let freeze for at least 90 minutes prior to eating. Defrost frozen yogurt for about 20 minutes before serving. Serve with Nutella.

Ice Cream

Chocolate Crisps Coffee Ice Cream

- ✓ 1 cup of heavy cream
- ✓ 1/2 cup condensed milk
- ✓ 2 tbsp. ground coffee
- ✓ 1 dark chocolate bar

Make some coffee: mix ground coffee with 1 cup of boiling water and left for 2-3 min. In a bowl combine heavy cream, coffee and condensed milk and whisk together until an airy cream. Put into glass form and let it in freezer for 30 min. After this put your ice cream into mixer bowl, turn on a slow speed and slowly add ground chocolate. Put it back in freezer and left for 6 - 12 hours. Serve in warm dish individually.

Simple Vanilla Ice Cream

- ✓ 1 cup heavy cream
- ✓ 1 quart half-and-half cream
- ✓ 1/2 cup sugar
- ✓ 2 tsp. vanilla extract
- ✓ 1 pinch salt

In a bowl combine all ingredients and whisk together until an airy cream. Place into glass form and put in the freezer for 20 min. Take it out and mix again with a whisk, and put it back. Repeat for a few more times and left for 6 - 12 hours. Serve in warm dish individually.

Drunk Avocado Ice Cream

- ✓ 1 big avocado
- ✓ 3 cups heavy cream
- ✓ 3 tbsp. White Rum
- ✓ 2 egg yolks
- ✓ 2 tsp. flour
- ✓ 1/4 cup sugar
- ✓ 1 tsp. vanilla extract
- ✓ a pinch of salt

Peel the avocado, cut into large pieces. Put in a bowl of a blender, add 1 glass of cream and mix, turning the avocado into a puree. Add rum and mix again until smooth. Put in the refrigerator for 2 hours. Whisk the yolks with 1 glass of cream. In a saucepan mix the flour, sugar and salt. Pour the remaining cream, mixing thoroughly. Put on medium heat and with constant stirring boil until mixture becomes thick. Add the hot mixture to the yolks, slowly mixing it. Put it back to pan and return it on fire for a minute.

Remove from heat, cool, add vanilla and mix. Put in the refrigerator for at least 30 minutes.

Combine the mixture with the avocado and egg mixture, pour in a glass form and put in a freezer. Take it out whisk it and put back into fridge for 6 - 12 hours.

Ricotta Hazelnut Ice Cream

- ✓ 1 1/2 cups milk
- ✓ 1 cup sugar
- ✓ 3 tbsp. butter
- ✓ 1 pound Ricotta
- ✓ 1/2 cup Dark Rum
- ✓ 1 1/2 pounds hazelnuts
- ✓ 1 tbsp. lemon zest

Blend hazelnuts in blender in very fine crumbs. In a saucepan combine milk and a quarter cup of sugar, put on a medium heat and stir until sugar dissolves.
In another large pot put butter, the remaining sugar, add rum and one glass of water. Put on a small fire and, whisking the mixture with a whisk.
Remove from heat, cool slightly, add ricotta, ground hazelnuts and lemon zest. Stir. Pour in the milk and sugar mixture and mix again thoroughly. Freeze in the freezer for 30 minutes. Take it out whisk it and put back into fridge for 6 - 12 hours.

Blueberry Ice Cream

- ✓ 3 cups frozen wild blueberries
- ✓ 3 cups of heavy cream
- ✓ 1 cup sugar
- ✓ 1/2 fresh lemon
- ✓ 1 tsp. cinnamon
- ✓ 1 tsp. vanilla extract

In a large saucepan, combine the blueberries with sugar and bring to a boil. Reduce heat and simmer, uncovered, until sugar is dissolved and the blueberries are softened. Strain a mixture, discard seeds and skin and let it chill. Add cream, lemon juice from ½ lemon, cinnamon and vanilla with blueberry syrup and whisk together until an airy cream. Freeze in the freezer for 30 minutes. Take it out whisk it and put back into fridge for 6 - 12 hours.

Fried Mexican Ice Cream

- ✓ 1 pint of vanilla ice cream (Use "Simple Vanilla Ice Cream" recipe)
- ✓ 2 eggs
- ✓ 1/2 tsp. vanilla extract
- ✓ 2 cups sweetened corn flakes
- ✓ 1 tsp. cinnamon grounded
- ✓ cooking oil for frying

Place 4 scoops (about 1/2 cup each) of ice cream in a small pan and put in freezer for 1 hour.
In a small mixing bowl stir together a half of an eggs and vanilla. At this time in a pie plate carefully stir together corn flakes and cinnamon. Dip each frozen ice cream ball in the egg mixture, and then roll them in the cereal. Return coated ice cream balls to freezer and freeze for 1 hour. After this remove ice cream balls out and repeat with other half of eggs and vanilla, and freeze again for several hours. In a deep fat fryer fry frozen coated ice cream balls in deep hot oil (375°F)

for 15 seconds or untill golden brown. Drain on paper towels; return the fried ice cream balls to freezer while frying the remaining balls. Let it chill and serve with whipped cream.

Pumpkin Ice Cream

- 1 can solid-pack pumpkin
- 1 cup heavy cream
- 2/3 cup half-and-half cream
- 2/3 cup sugar
- 1 tsp. vanilla extract
- 1 tsp. cinnamon
- 1/2 tsp. ginger ginger
- 1/8 tsp. nutmeg
- 1/8 tsp. cloves

Ground cloves in blender and great nutmeg. Add pumpkin and mix until smooth. Put heavy cream, half-and-half cream and sugar in a large bowl and whisk until sugar dissolves. Combine cream and your pumpkin mixture, add vanilla and cinnamon and whisk more until airy cream. Place in the freezer for 30 minutes. Take it out whisk it and put back into fridge for 6 - 12 hours more. Serve with chopped crackers.

Green Tea Ice Cream

- ✓ 1 cup milk
- ✓ 2 egg yolks
- ✓ 4 tbsp. sugar
- ✓ 1 cup heavy cream
- ✓ 2 tbsp. green tea (Matcha)
- ✓ 1/2 cup hot water
- ✓ 1 tbsp. pistachios

Lightly whisk egg yolks in a pan. Add milk and sugar to the pan and mix well. Put the pan on low heat and heat the mixture, stirring constantly. When the mixture thickens, remove from the heat. Soak the bottom of the pan in ice water and cool the mixture. Mix hot water and green tea powder together. Add the green tea to the egg mixture and mix well. Let it cool and add heavy cream to mixture and mix until airy consistency. Put mixture in a glass form and place in the freezer for 30 minutes. Ground pistachios in blender.Take the form out whisk it, add pistachios and put back into fridge for 6 - 12 hours more. Serve with whole pistachios.

Vegetarian Banana Ice Cream

- ✓ 4 ripe bananas
- ✓ 3 tbsp. lemon juice
- ✓ 3/4 cup simple syrup
- ✓ 1 cup almond milk
- ✓ 2 tbsp. cocoa powder

Slice bananas, put them in a container and place it in the freezer for five hours or overnight. Put the frozen bananas in a food processor, add syrup and milk. Blend the mixture until it resembles soft serve ice cream. Then when it's blended add two tablespoons cocoa powder. Blend it again until the cocoa powder is mixed in. Put mixture in a glass bowl and place into freezer for 5-6 hours.

Salted Caramel Ice Cream

- ✓ 2 cups milk
- ✓ 1 1/2 cups sugar
- ✓ 1 tbsp. salted butter
- ✓ 3 egg yolks
- ✓ 2 tbsp. flour
- ✓ pinch of salt
- ✓ 1 cup heavy cream
- ✓ 1 1/2 vanilla extract
- ✓ 1 tsp. sea salt

First you need to make caramel. In a small saucepan boil the milk over medium heat. Turn off the fire, but leave it on the stove to save warm. Pour sugar into the saucepan, stirring, bring it to a golden color. Fry the sugar until it melt and change color to light brown. Then add butter and mix until uniform. Add warm milk into mixture and stir with whip. While preparing caramel, mix the yolks, milk, flour and salt in a bowl and whisk a bit. When caramel-milk mixture becomes homogeneous, begin to gradually combine, whisking, two mixtures between each other. Add caramel to egg small portion, about a quarter cup at a time, whisking well after each addition. When the two mixtures are mixed, put them on a weak fire and continue beating whisk while heating, for about 5 minutes. Remove from heat and through a sieve pour into a dry clean bowl. Allow the mixture to cool. Whip cream with vanilla to elastic peaks and put in the freezer for 4 hours, or overnight. Mix all your mixtures, put in a glass form and place in the freezer for 30 minutes. Take the form out whisk it and put back into fridge for 30 minutes more. Repeat whisking few more times, add sea salt and left in a freezer for 5-6 hours. Serve covered with pinch of sea salt.

Gelato

Berry Mint Gelato

- ✓ 2 cups whole milk
- ✓ 1/2 cup heavy cream
- ✓ 4 big egg yolks
- ✓ 1 cup sugar
- ✓ 1/2 tsp. vanilla
- ✓ 1 cup fresh blackberries
- ✓ 1 cup fresh raspberries
- ✓ 1 tsp. mint extract

Blend berries in a food processor, then transfer this mixture into a saucepan, add mint extract and cook for 10-15 minutes. Discard seeds using a sieve and let the berry mixture cool.

Mix milk and heavy cream in a saucepan, add half of sugar. Cook over low heat to dissolve sugar; do not boil it, keep the milk mixture hot. In a bowl, beat the egg yolks with rest of sugar until pale yellow and thick for about 2 minutes. Add vanilla. Pour egg mix into the saucepan with milk; do it slowly and carefully to prevent coagulating yolks and forming lumps.

Cook over very low heat stirring constantly. Pour in the berry mixture and keep stirring until blended well. Let it cool.
End process in the ice cream machine according to instructions, or pour it into a covered container and refrigerate least 4 hours or overnight. Garnish with fresh mint leaves and berries.

Limoncello Gelato

- ✓ 2 cups whole milk
- ✓ 1/2 cup heavy cream
- ✓ 4 big egg yolks
- ✓ 1 cup sugar
- ✓ 1/2 tsp. vanilla
- ✓ 3 tbsp. Limoncello liqueur
- ✓ 1 tbsp. lemon zest
- ✓ 1 tbsp. mint extract

Mix milk and heavy cream in a saucepan, add half of sugar. Cook over low heat to dissolve sugar; do not boil it, keep the milk mixture hot. In a bowl, beat the egg yolks with rest of sugar until pale yellow and thick for about 2 minutes. Add vanilla. Pour egg mix into the saucepan with milk; do it slowly and carefully to prevent coagulating yolks and forming lumps. Cook over very low heat stirring constantly. Add Limoncello,

lemon juice and zest and keep stirring until blended well. Let it cool.
End process in the ice cream machine according to instructions, or pour it into a covered container and refrigerate least 4 hours or overnight. Garnish with lemon slices.

Honey Gelato

- ✓ 2 cups whole milk
- ✓ 1/2 cup heavy cream
- ✓ 4 big egg yolks
- ✓ 1/2 cup sugar
- ✓ 1/2 cup honey melted
- ✓ 1/2 tsp. cinnamon
- ✓ 1/2 tsp. nutmeg
- ✓ 1 clove

Mix milk and heavy cream in a saucepan, cook over low heat to make the milk mixture hot. Add clove. In a bowl, beat the egg yolks with sugar until pale yellow and thick for about 2 minutes. Pour egg mix into the saucepan with milk; do it slowly and carefully to prevent coagulating yolks and forming lumps. Cook over very low heat stirring constantly. Discard clove, add

honey, cinnamon and nutmeg; and keep stirring until blended well. Let it cool.
End process in the ice cream machine according to instructions, or pour it into a covered container and refrigerate least 4 hours or overnight.

Coconut Banana Gelato

- ✓ 2 cups whole milk
- ✓ 1/2 cup coconut cream
- ✓ 4 big egg yolks
- ✓ 1 cup sugar
- ✓ 2 very ripe bananas, peeled and quartered
- ✓ 2 tbsp. lemon juice
- ✓ 1 tsp. vanilla

Blend bananas in a food processor, add lemon juice and mix thoroughly.
Mix milk and coconut cream in a saucepan, add half of sugar. Cook over low heat to dissolve sugar; do not boil it, keep the milk mixture hot. In a bowl, beat the egg yolks with rest of sugar until pale yellow and thick for about 2 minutes.
Pour egg mix into the saucepan with milk; do it slowly and carefully to prevent coagulating yolks and forming lumps. Cook over very low heat stirring constantly. Add bananas and vanilla; keep stirring until blended well. Let it cool.
End process in the ice cream machine according to instructions, or pour it into a covered container and refrigerate least 4 hours or overnight.

Tiramisu Gelato

- ✓ 2 cups whole milk
- ✓ 1/2 cup heavy cream
- ✓ 4 big egg yolks
- ✓ 1 cup sugar
- ✓ 1 tsp. vanilla
- ✓ 1 cup soft mascarpone cheese
- ✓ 1/2 cup coffee liqueur
- ✓ cocoa powder (to garnish)

Mix milk and heavy cream in a saucepan, add half of sugar. Cook over low heat to dissolve sugar; do not boil it, keep the milk mixture hot. In a bowl, beat the egg yolks with rest of sugar until pale yellow and thick for about 2 minutes. Pour egg mix into the saucepan with milk; do it slowly and carefully to prevent coagulating yolks and forming lumps. Cook over very

low heat stirring constantly. Combine mascarpone cheese, coffee liqueur and vanilla. Add it into the saucepan with milk mix; keep stirring until blended well. Let it cool.
End process in the ice cream machine according to instructions, or pour it into a covered container and refrigerate least 4 hours or overnight. Dust Tiramisu Gelato with cocoa powder before serving.

Coffee Gelato with Orange

- ✓ 2 cups whole milk
- ✓ 1/2 cup heavy cream
- ✓ 4 big egg yolks
- ✓ 1 cup sugar
- ✓ 1 tsp. vanilla
- ✓ 2 portions freshly brewed espresso
- ✓ 1/2 cup coffee liqueur
- ✓ 1 tbsp. orange zest
- ✓ 1/3 tsp. orange extract
- ✓ bittersweet chocolate, shaved

Mix milk and heavy cream in a saucepan, add half of sugar. Cook over low heat to dissolve sugar; do not boil it, keep the milk mixture hot. In a bowl, beat the egg yolks with rest of sugar until pale yellow and thick for about 2 minutes. Pour egg mix into the saucepan with milk; do it slowly and carefully to prevent coagulating yolks and forming lumps. Cook over very low heat stirring constantly. Add vanilla, espresso, coffee liqueur, orange extract and zest and keep stirring until blended well. Let it cool.

End process in the ice cream machine according to instructions, or pour it into a covered container and refrigerate least 4 hours or overnight. Garnish with bittersweet chocolate.

Choco-Choco Gelato

- ✓ 2 cups whole milk
- ✓ 1/2 cup heavy cream
- ✓ 4 big egg yolks
- ✓ 1 cup brown sugar
- ✓ 1 tsp. vanilla
- ✓ 1 cup semi-sweet chocolate chips
- ✓ Chocolate syrup

Mix milk and heavy cream in a saucepan, add half of sugar and chocolate chips. Cook over low heat to dissolve sugar; do not boil it, keep the milk mixture hot. In a bowl, beat the egg yolks with rest of sugar until pale yellow and thick for about 2 minutes. Pour egg mix into the saucepan with milk; do it slowly and carefully to prevent coagulating yolks and forming lumps. Cook over very low heat stirring constantly.
End process in the ice cream machine according to instructions, or pour it into a covered container and refrigerate least 4 hours or overnight. Garnish with chocolate syrup.

Caramel Gelato with White Chocolate

- ✓ 2 cups whole milk
- ✓ 1/2 cup heavy cream
- ✓ 4 big egg yolks
- ✓ 1/2 cup sugar
- ✓ 1 cup white chocolate chips

for caramel syrup:
- ✓ 1/2 cup sugar
- ✓ 1/4 cup water
- ✓ 1 tbsp. lemon juice
- ✓ 1/2 tsp. vanilla

Mix milk and heavy cream in a saucepan, cook over low heat to make the milk mixture hot. In a bowl, beat the egg yolks with sugar until pale yellow and thick for about 2 minutes. Pour egg mix into the saucepan with milk; do it slowly and carefully to prevent coagulating yolks and forming lumps. Cook over very low heat stirring constantly. Let it cool; add white chocolate chips and mix well.

Cook easy caramel syrup: in glass bowl mix sugar and water, add lemon juice and vanilla. boil in the microwave for 3-5 minutes until golden color.

End gelato process in the ice cream machine according to instructions, or pour it into a covered container and refrigerate least 4 hours or overnight. Garnish with caramel syrup.

Melon Gelato with Amaretto

- ✓ 2 cups whole milk
- ✓ 1/2 cup heavy cream
- ✓ 4 big egg yolks
- ✓ 1 cup sugar
- ✓ 2 ripe melon or cantaloupe, peeled and chopped
- ✓ 1/3 cup light corn syrup
- ✓ 2 teaspoons lemon juice
- ✓ 2 tbsp. Amaretto
- ✓ 1 teaspoon vanilla

Blend melon in a food processor, add lemon juice, vanilla, corn syrup and Amaretto; mix thoroughly.
Mix milk and coconut cream in a saucepan, add half of sugar. Cook over low heat to dissolve sugar; do not boil it, keep the milk mixture hot. In a bowl, beat the egg yolks with rest of sugar until pale yellow and thick for about 2 minutes.
Pour egg mix into the saucepan with milk; do it slowly and carefully to prevent coagulating yolks and forming lumps.

Cook over very low heat stirring constantly. Add melon mixture; keep stirring until blended well. Let it cool.
End process in the ice cream machine according to instructions, or pour it into a covered container and refrigerate least 4 hours or overnight.

Spicy Cinnamon Gelato

- ✓ 2 cups whole milk
- ✓ 1/2 cup heavy cream
- ✓ 4 big egg yolks
- ✓ 1 cup brown sugar
- ✓ 4 cinnamon sticks
- ✓ 1/2 teaspoon chili powder

Mix milk and coconut cream in a saucepan, add half of sugar and cinnamon sticks. Cook over low heat to dissolve sugar; do not boil it, keep the milk mixture hot. In a bowl, beat the egg yolks with rest of sugar until pale yellow and thick for about 2 minutes.

Remove cinnamon sticks and pour egg mix into the saucepan with milk; do it slowly and carefully to prevent coagulating yolks and forming lumps. Cook over very low heat stirring constantly. Add chili powder; keep stirring until blended well. Let it cool.

Sorbets

Fresh Green Apple Sorbet

- ✓ 1.6 lb. granny smith apples, unpeeled, cored, and quartered
- ✓ juice of 1/2 a lemon
- ✓ 1 cup water
- ✓ 1 1/2 heaped cups caster sugar
- ✓ 3 tsp. calvados, optional
- ✓ 1/8 tsp. liquid green food coloring, optional

Place the apples in a saucepan along with lemon juice, water, and sugar over high heat. Bring to the boil, then reduce to a simmer. Cook the apples about 20 minutes. Remove from the heat and cool to room temperature. Then, place them to a blender and puree the apple mixture until smooth. Strain the mixture through a fine sieve. Stir through the calvados and green food coloring. Refrigerate the apple mixture until cold. Remove the mixture from the fridge and churn in an ice cream machine according to the manufacture's instructions. Once frozen, transfer the sorbet to a container, cover tightly, and place in the freezer for a minimum of 4 hours.

Pineapple Daiquiri Sorbet

- ✓ 4 Cups fresh pineapple, chunks
- ✓ 1/2 cup superfine sugar
- ✓ 4 tbsp. light rum
- ✓ 2 tbsp. lime juice

Place pineapple, sugar, rum and lime juice into a blender and blend until smooth. Transfer mixture in the refrigerator and cool for one hour. Pour mixture into a frozen canister for your ice cream maker, and process about 20 minutes. Serve immediately. Enjoy!

Mojito Sorbet

- ✓ 1 cup water
- ✓ 1 cup sugar
- ✓ 1/2 cup mint leaves
- ✓ 1/4 cup grated lime zest
- ✓ 1 cup lime juice
- ✓ 1 1/2 cups citrus-flavored sparkling water
- ✓ 2 tbsp. rum (optional)

Heat the water, sugar, and mint leaves in a saucepan over medium heat. Bring the mixture to a boil, reduce heat, and simmer for 3 to 5 minutes to extract the mint flavor. Cool the mixture, and strain out the mint leaves. In a bowl mix the cooled mint mixture, add lime zest, lime juice, sparkling water, and rum. Pour into the container of an ice cream maker, and freeze according to the manufacturer's instructions. Freeze in a sealed container for a harder sorbet.

Sweet Tomato-Basil Sorbet

- ✓ 1 cup sugar
- ✓ 3 lb. ripe tomatoes, peeled, cored, and cut into chunks
- ✓ 6 tbsp. minced fresh basil leaves

In a saucepan over high heat, bring sugar and water to a boil. Cool about 15 minutes. Meanwhile, purée tomatoes in a blender. Rub through a fine strainer into a bowl. Combine syrup, tomato purée, and basil. Freeze in an ice cream maker until dasher is hard to turn. Freeze sorbet at least 3 hours.

Mint Espresso Sorbet

- ✓ 1 cup mint leaves, chopped
- ✓ 1/4 tsp. pure vanilla extract
- ✓ 1/4 cup freshly brewed espresso
- ✓ 2 1/4 cups of water
- ✓ 1/2 cup sugar
- ✓ pinch of salt

In a saucepan over medium heat, bring the chopped mint, half the water, salt and sugar to a simmer. Cover the pan, lower the heat slightly, and cook for about 3 minutes, until the sugar is dissolved. Remove from the heat, and add the vanilla and espresso, and stir. Stir in the remaining water. Transfer the mixture to a bowl, and cool in the refrigerator until cold, about an hour. When cooled, freeze in your ice cream maker according to the manufacturer's instructions.

Strawberry Balsamic Sorbet

- ✓ 3⁄4 cup balsamic vinegar
- ✓ 4 cups strawberries, hulled and halved, plus
- ✓ 4 strawberries, coarsely chopped
- ✓ 1 tbsp. Honey

In a small saucepan, bring the vinegar to a boil over medium-low heat. Cook about 5 minutes. It must reduce by half. Remove from heat and cool. Place the halved strawberries in a blender. Puree until very smooth. Pass the puree through a fine-mesh sieve. Add the balsamic reduction and honey to the puree and stir to combine. Refrigerate until cold. Freeze the mixture in an ice-cream maker according to manufacturer's instructions. Spoon into special bowls and garnish with the chopped strawberries. You can store in the freezer for up to 2 days.

Romantic Lavender Sorbet

- ✓ 2 1/2 cups water
- ✓ 1/2 cup sugar
- ✓ 4 lavender flowers (4 heads pesticide-free)
- ✓ 1/4 cup lemon juice (or juice of 1 lemon)

Combine 1 cup of water and the sugar in a saucepan over medium heat. Bring the mixture to a simmer, stirring, and cook the syrup until it is clear. After approximately 10 minutes, remove from the heat and let cool completely. In a large saucepan, combine 1 cup of the syrup with the lavender flowers and the lemon juice. Stirring constantly, bring the mixture to a boil over medium-high heat. Remove from the heat and let cool completely. Add the remaining 1 1/2 cups water. Transfer the mixture to an ice-cream machine and freeze according to the manufacturer's instructions. Let the sorbet stand in the refrigerator for 10 minutes before serving. Garnish with the fresh lavender flowers and serve.

Grapefruit'n'Rum Sorbet

- ✓ 1 big ripe grapefruit, peeles and chopped
- ✓ 1 cup sugar
- ✓ 1 cup water
- ✓ 3 tbsp. light rum
- ✓ 2 tbsp. strained lemon juice
- ✓ 1/2 tsp. vanilla extract

Place grapefruit into saucepan with sugar, water and lemon juice. Bring to the boil. Simmer 10 minutes, mashing as they cook. Set aside and cool. Put through a fine strainer. Let cool to room temperature. Stir in vanilla and rum. Refrigerate several hours, or overnight. Transfer to ice cream freezer and freeze according to manufacturer's directions. Freeze 1-2 hours before serving.

Cherry Vanilla Sorbet

- ✓ 5 cups black cherries, pitted
- ✓ 1 cup water
- ✓ 1/2 cup sugar
- ✓ 1 tbsp. vanilla extract, pure

Place sugar and water into a saucepan and place over medium-high heat. Bring mixture to a boil. Continue to boil until a thin, syrup consistency is reached. Add vanilla extract. Cool the mixture. Then pour into a separate container and refrigerate for 2 hours. Place cherries and syrup in a food processor. Puree until mixture is smooth and frothy. Strain mixture to separate cherry skins to reach a smoother consistency. Repeat if necessary. Transfer mixture into the freezer tub of your ice cream maker and follow the manufacturers instructions for freezing. Freeze sorbet for 3-5 hours.

Summer Citrus Sorbet

- ✓ 1 cup water
- ✓ 1 cup sugar
- ✓ 3 cups grapefruit juice

Mix the water and sugar together in a pan over a low heat, and bring up to boil until the sugar dissolves. Let the syrup to boil for 4 minutes. Remove from heat and cool. Combine the citrus juice and the cooled syrup. Freeze in an ice cream machine according to manufacturer's directions. Garnish with mint leaves.

Granita

Green Tea Granita

- ✓ 4 green tea bags
- ✓ 4 cups water for tea
- ✓ 1 cup water for syrup
- ✓ 3 tbsp. lemon juice
- ✓ 1/2 cup sugar or honey
- ✓ lemon slices

Make some tea: place tea bags in a large bowl, add boiling water and let it steep for 10-15 minutes. When time goes off remove tea bags. Combine 1 cup of water, sugar, lemon juice in a saucepan and bring it to boil. Mix tea and sugar syrup, and let cool to room temperature. Transfer it into the fridge and freeze until slightly firm (about 1 hour). Remove tea mixture from freezer and beat with wire whisk to break ice crystals, repeat this process 2-3 times until ice is granular. You can also freeze tea firm and scrape it with a fork until fluffy.
Garnish with lemon slices.

Citrus Ginger Granita

- 1 cup fresh lemon juice
- 1 cup fresh orange juice
- 1 cup water
- 1 tbsp. lemon zest, grated
- 1/2 tbsp. orange zest, grated
- 1/2 tsp. ginger, grated
- 1/4 cup sugar
- lemon or orange slices

Combine 1 cup of water and sugar in a saucepan and bring it to boil, let cool to room temperature. Mix lemon and orange juices in a big bowl, add zest, ginger and sugar syrup. Transfer the bowl it in the freeze until slightly firm (about 1 hour). After time passes remove citrus mixture from freezer and beat with wire whisk to break ice crystals, repeat this process 2-3 times until ice is granular or freeze mixture firm and scrape it with a fork until fluffy. Garnish with lemon or orange slices. If citrus are too sour - add more sugar syrup.

Watermelon Granita

- 1 middle sweet watermelon
- 1 cup water
- 1/2 cup sugar
- 2 tbsp. fresh lemon juice
- 2 tsp. fresh mint leaves, finely chopped

Combine 1 cup of water and sugar in a saucepan and bring it to boil, let cool to room temperature. Remove the rinds from the watermelon and cut the it into chunks. Transfer watermelon into a blender, add simple sugar syrup, lemon juice and mint. Puree it all together and pour the mixture into a baking dish or big bowl. Freeze until slightly firm (about 1 hour). After time passes remove watermelon mixture from freezer and beat with wire whisk to break ice crystals, repeat this process 2-3 times until ice is granular or freeze mixture firm and scrape it with a fork until fluffy. Serve with fresh mint leaves.

Strawberry Basil Granita

- ✓ 3 cups strawberries, hulled and chopped
- ✓ 1 cup water
- ✓ 1/4 cup lime juice
- ✓ 3 tbsp. honey
- ✓ 2 tbsp. red basil leaves, finely chopped

Put strawberries into a blender, add honey, lime juice and basil. Puree it all together and pour the mixture into a baking dish or big bowl. Freeze until slightly firm (about 1 hour). After time passes remove strawberry mixture from freezer and beat with wire whisk to break ice crystals, repeat this process 2-3 times until ice is granular or freeze mixture firm and scrape it with a fork until fluffy. Serve with fresh basil leaves.

Cappuccino Granita

- 3 cups freshly brewed extra strong coffee
- 1 cup heavy cream
- 1 cup hot water
- 1/2 cup sugar
- 1/2 tsp. ground cinnamon
- 1/4 tsp. ground nutmeg
- whipped cream and chocolate to garnish

Combine warm coffee with hot water and sugar, stir until sugar is dissolved, let it cool. Add in coffee mixture heavy cream, ground cinnamon and nutmeg. Transfer into a baking dish and Freeze until slightly firm (about 1 hour). After time passes remove cappuccino mixture from freezer and beat with wire whisk to break ice crystals, repeat this process 2-3 times until ice is granular or freeze mixture firm and scrape it with a fork until fluffy. Garnish with whipped cream and chocolate (shavings or syrup).

Peach Granita

- 3 cups ripe peaches, peeled and sliced
- 1 cup wine (can be replaced with water)
- 1/2 cup sugar
- 2 tbsp. fresh lemon juice
- 1/2 tsp. vanilla extract
- 2 lemongrass stems, finely chopped, plus extra to serve

Combine 1 cup of wine (or water) and sugar in a saucepan and bring it to boil, let cool to room temperature. Put peaches into a blender, add sugar syrup, lemon juice, vanilla extract and lemongrass. Puree it all together and pour the mixture into a baking dish or big bowl. Freeze until slightly firm (about 1 hour). After time passes remove peach mixture from freezer and beat with wire whisk to break ice crystals, repeat this process 2-3 times until ice is granular or freeze mixture firm and scrape it with a fork until fluffy. Garnish with fresh lemongrass stalks.

Champagne Granita

- ✓ 2 cups dry champagne or prosecco
- ✓ 1 cup water
- ✓ 1 tbsp. rose water
- ✓ 4 tbsp. vanilla sugar

Combine 1 cup of water and vanilla sugar in a saucepan and bring it to boil, let cool to room temperature. Mix champagne with sugar syrup, add rose water and and pour the mixture into a baking dish or big bowl. Freeze until slightly firm (about 1 hour). After time passes remove granita from freezer and beat with wire whisk to break ice crystals, repeat this process 2-3 times until ice is granular or freeze mixture firm and scrape it with a fork until fluffy. Serve with fresh mint leaves.

Margarita Granita

- 2 cups water
- 1/2 cup sugar
- 1/4 cup fresh lime juice
- 1/4 cup fresh lemon juice
- 3 tbsp. triple sec
- 1/4 cup silver agave tequila (may not be used to make a non alcoholic granita)
- 1 tsp. lime zest, grated
- salt and lime wedge for serving

Add water and sugar to a saucepan and bring it to boil until sugar is dissolved; let it cool. Mix sugar syrup with rest of the ingredients and pour the mixture into a baking dish or big bowl. Freeze until slightly firm. After time passes remove granita from freezer and beat with wire whisk to break ice crystals, repeat this process 2-3 times until ice is granular or freeze mixture firm and scrape it with a fork until fluffy. Rub the rims of 2 martini glasses with a lime wedge; dip the rims in salt. Serve granita in martini glasses.
You can also use ready margarita mix.

Pinacolada Granita

- ✓ 2 cups unsweetened pineapple juice
- ✓ 1 cup Coco Lopez coconut milk
- ✓ 1 cup sugar
- ✓ 1/2 cup white rum (may not be used to make a non alcoholic granita)
- ✓ 3/4 tsp. almond extract
- ✓ pineapple slice to garnish

Combine pineapple juice and sugar in a saucepan and bring it to boil, let cool to room temperature. Blend in blender sweet pineapple juice, coconut milk, rum and almond extract. Pour Pinacolada into a baking dish or big bowl. Freeze until slightly firm. After time passes remove granita from freezer and beat with wire whisk to break ice crystals, repeat this process 2-3 times until ice is granular or freeze mixture firm and scrape it with a fork until fluffy. Pour into a hurricane glass and garnish with pineapple slice.

Chocolate Mint Granita

- ✓ 1/2 cup unsweetened cocoa powder
- ✓ 3 cups water
- ✓ 1/2 cup sugar
- ✓ 1/2 tsp. vanilla
- ✓ 1/2 cup Hershey's Chocolate Syrup
- ✓ 2 tsp. fresh mint leaves, finely chopped
- ✓ whipped cream

Combine water, sugar, and cocoa powder and vanilla in a medium saucepan, cook until sugar is dissolved; let it cool. Add chocolate Syrup and mint, then pour the mixture into a baking dish or big bowl. Freeze until slightly firm. After time passes remove granita from freezer and beat with wire whisk to break ice crystals, repeat this process 2-3 times until ice is granular or freeze mixture firm and scrape it with a fork until fluffy. Serve with whipped cream, garnish with mint leaves.

Credits

Copyright © 2017 by Susan Moure – All right reserved

All legal rights reserved. You cannot offer this book for free or sell it. You do
not have reselling legal rights to this book. This eBook may not be recreated in
any file format or physical format without having the expressed written
approval. All Violators will be sued.
While efforts have been made to assess that the information contained in this
book is valid, neither the author nor the publisher assumes any accountability
for errors, interpretations, omissions or usage of the subject matters herein

Printed in Great Britain
by Amazon